MARIE'S MINIS

Pocket Size Coloring Book, Volume 1

I0467733

MARIE KAYE

INTRODUCTION

Thanks for entering into this adventure in coloring. I am
looking forward to sharing my love and passion for artistic
coloring with you.

I created all of the 50 images in this book by hand using my
own personal collection of photos taken by myself as
inspiration. I then used various symmetry software tools to
complete the overall designs you see here.

Although the images are copyrighted, as the buyer of this
book, please feel free to copy them for your personal use.
If you choose to do so, this will keep the book new and
ready for use. Some folks prefer to color on a heavier
paper so that the color from marker pens will not bleed
through the paper. I'll often color on 80lb paper. Each image is
on only one side of the page, the reverse side being left blank.

If you'd rather color right inside the book, I'd recommend
using a thin piece of cardboard behind your page, just to
protect the next image from any color bleeding through to the
next page, especially if you plan to use marker pens for
coloring. This will keep your images clean for you to work on.

The designs are suitable from beginning to advanced
students. The important thing is . . . HAVE FUN!
Don't forget to check out my other books in the HEARTS
AND FLORALS series. I am dedicated to producing these
designs for you.
- Marie Kaye

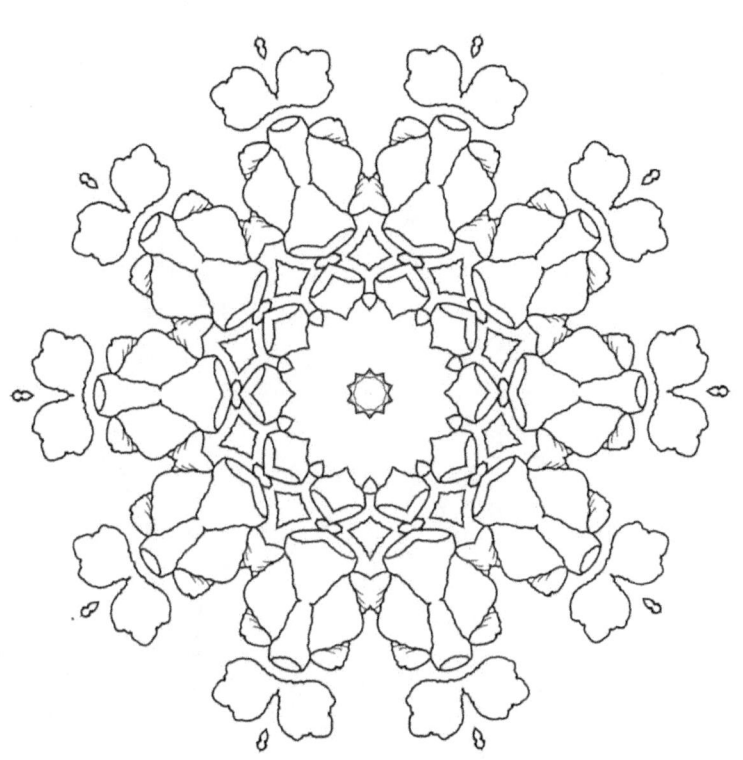

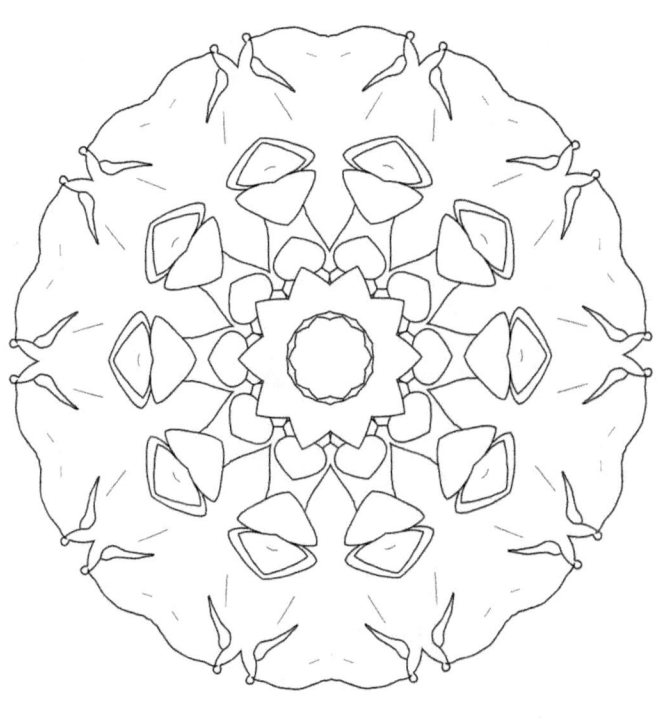

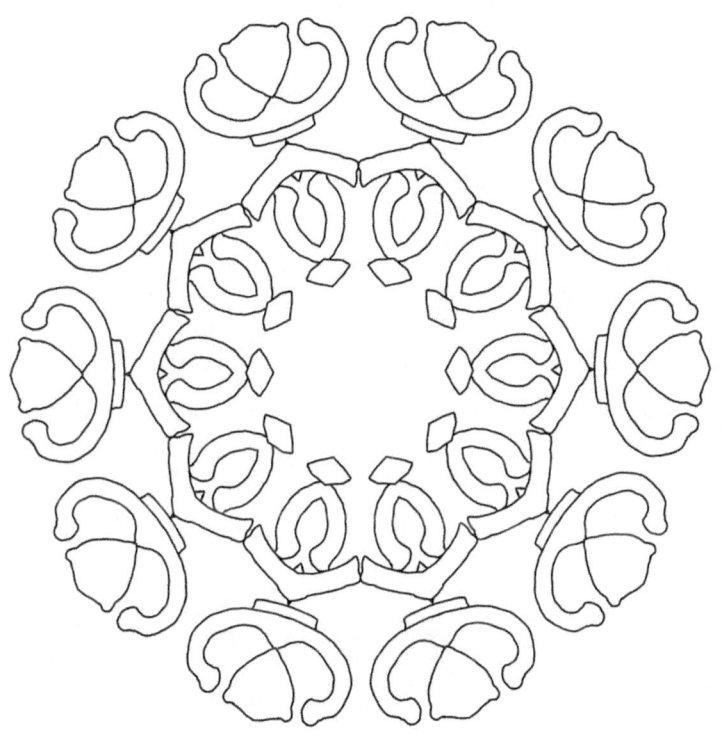

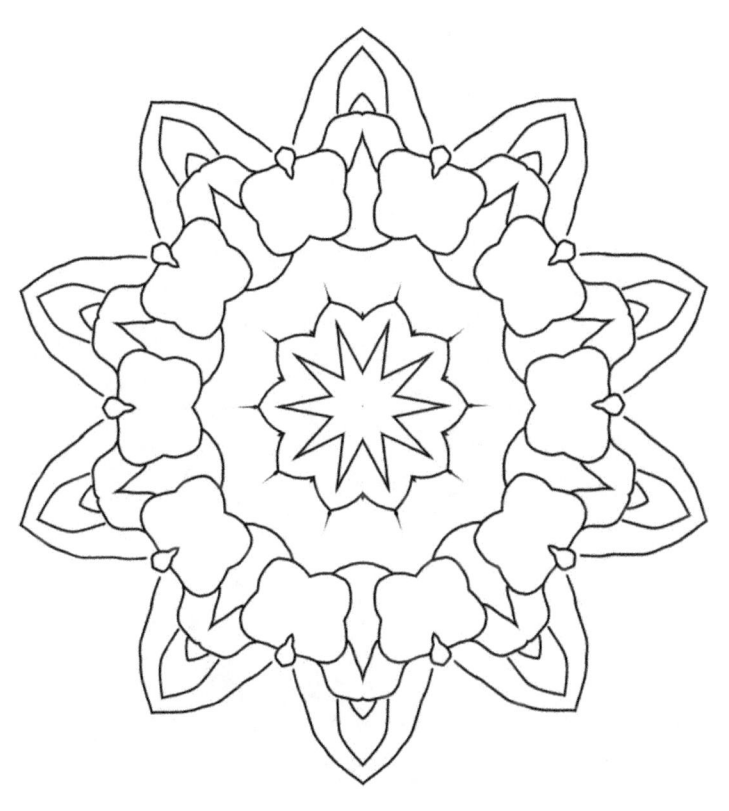

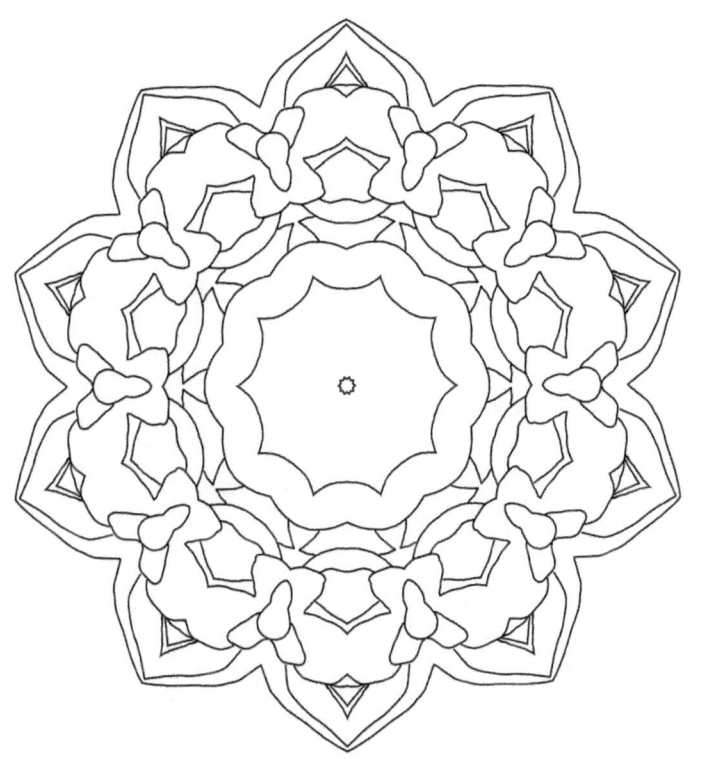

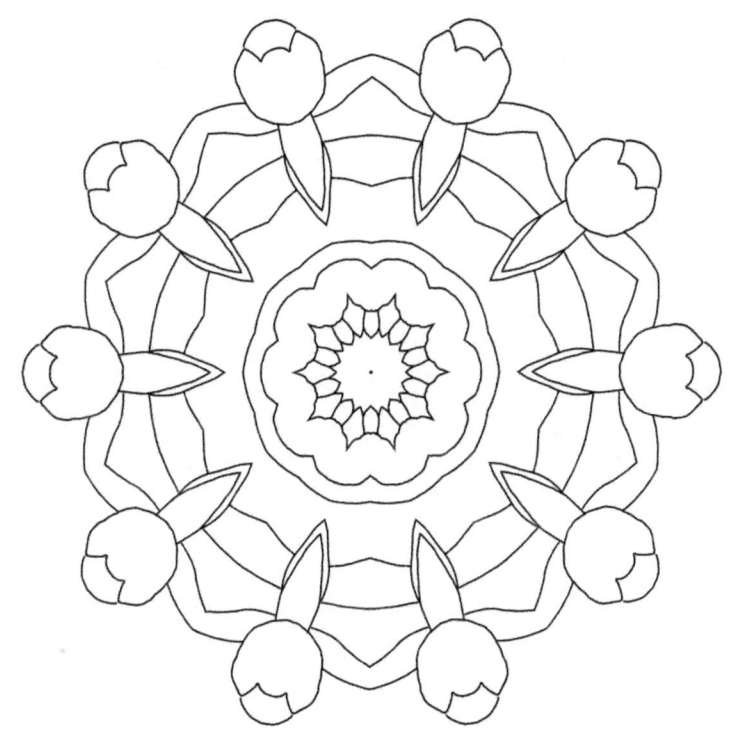

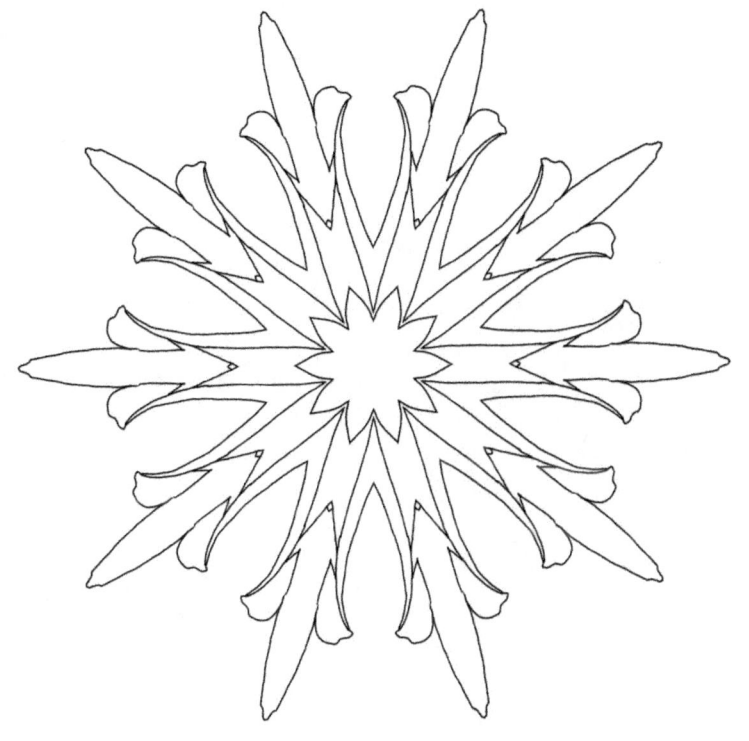

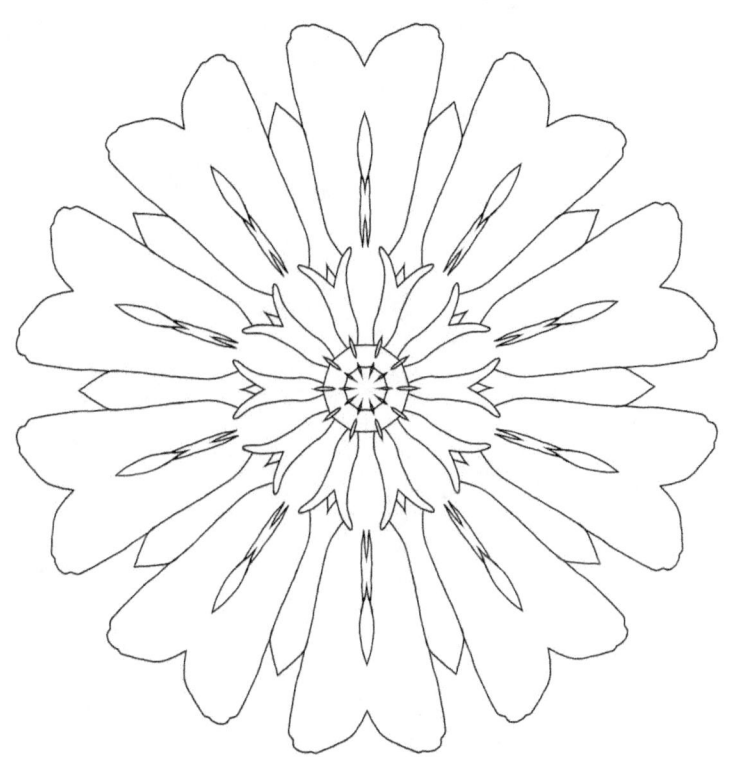

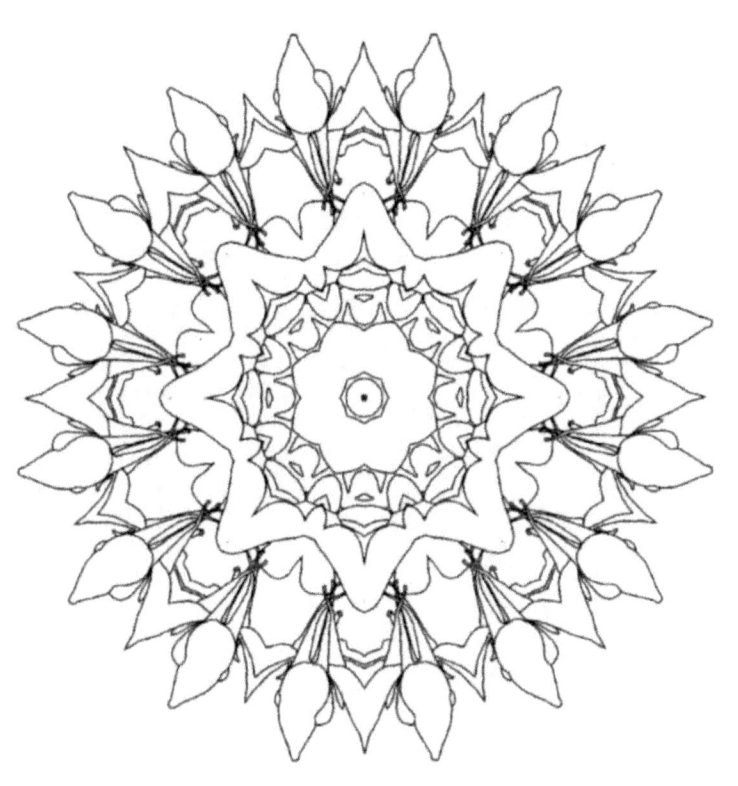

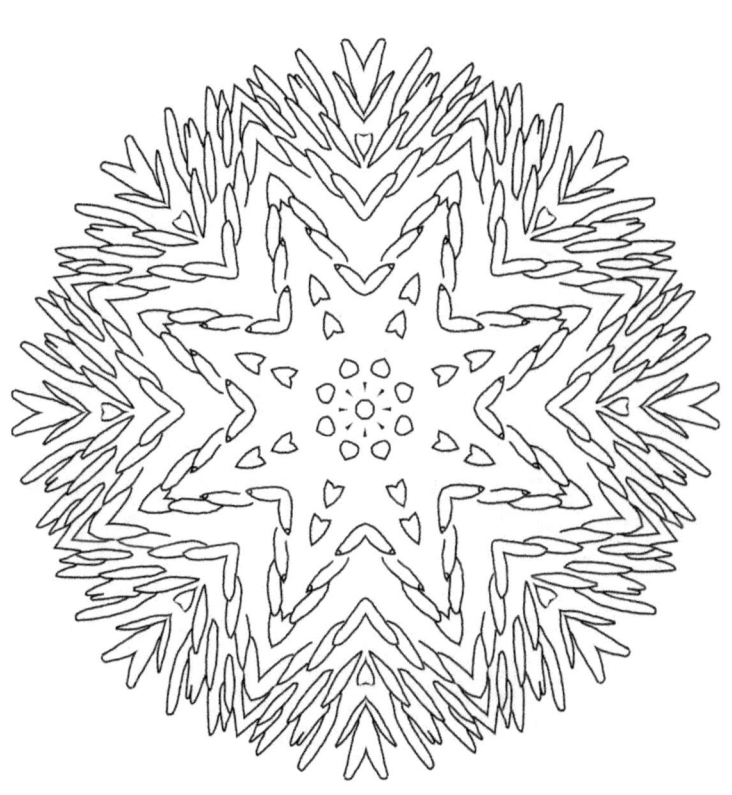

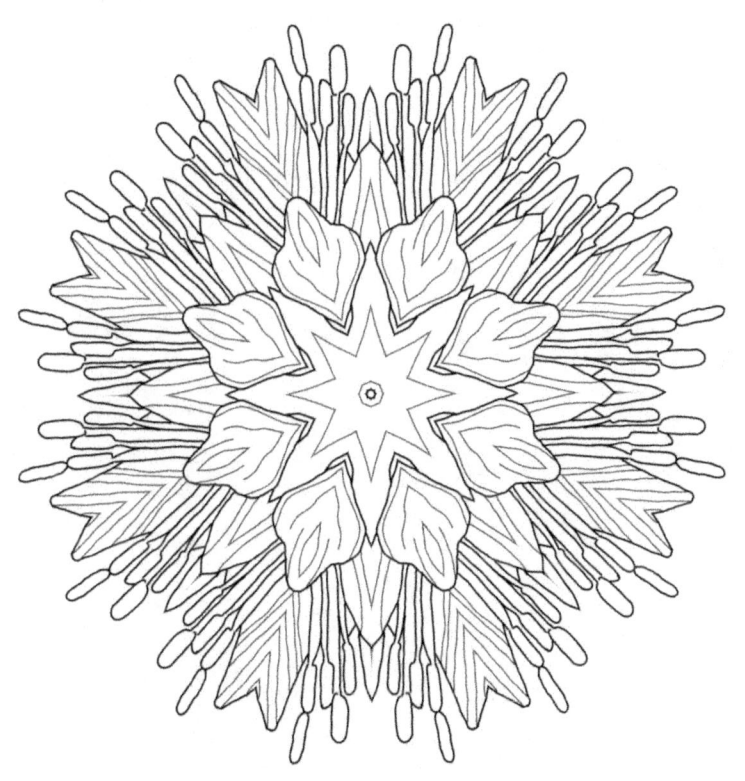

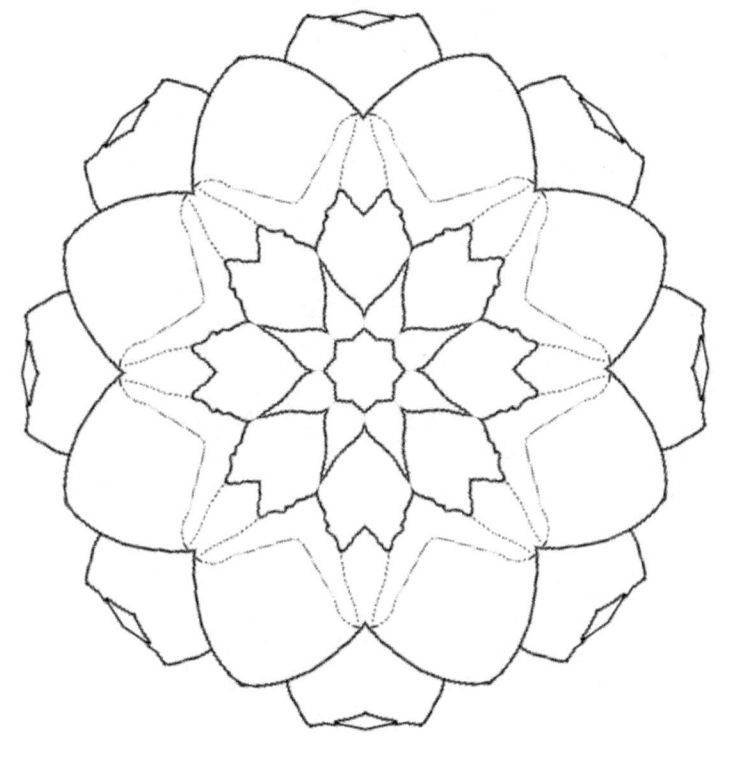

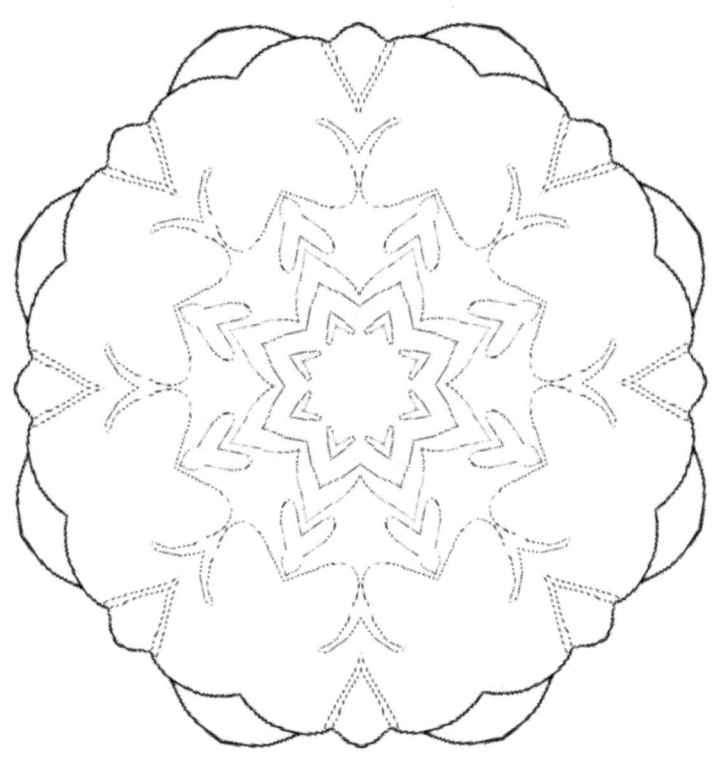

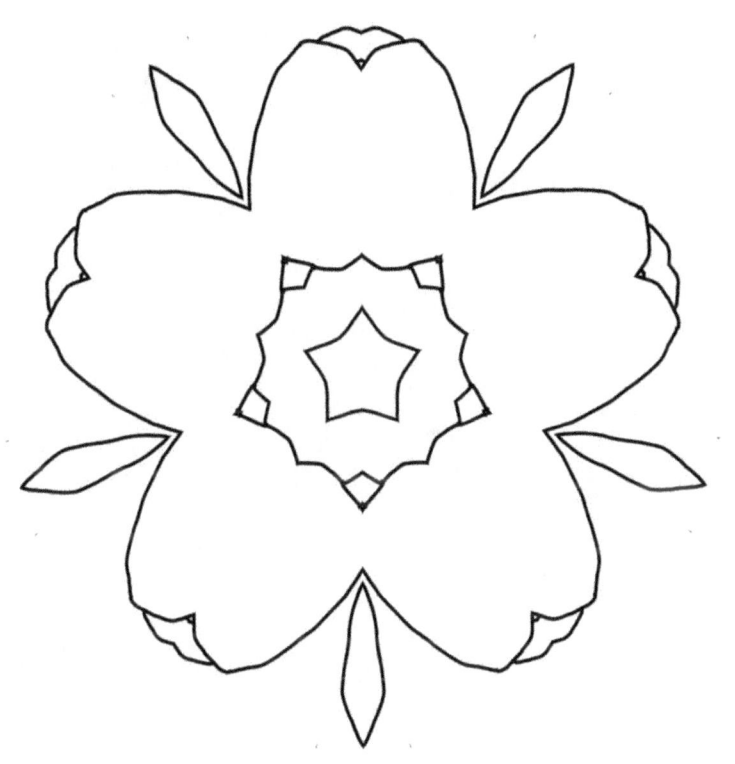

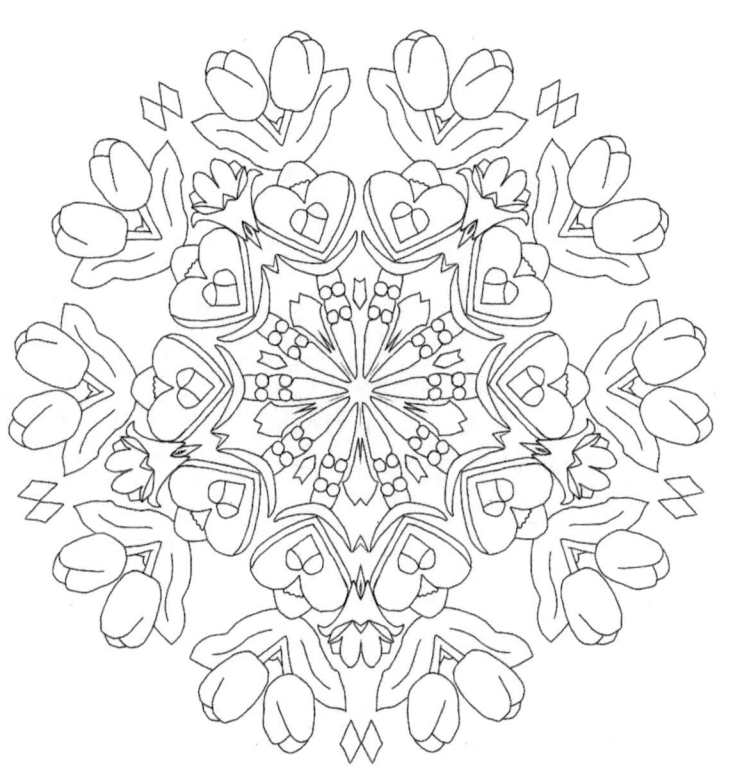

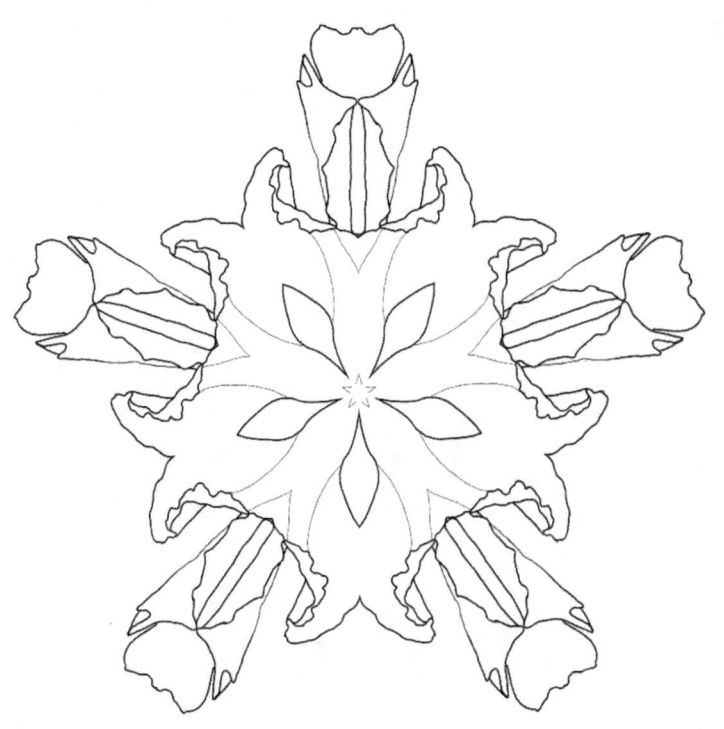

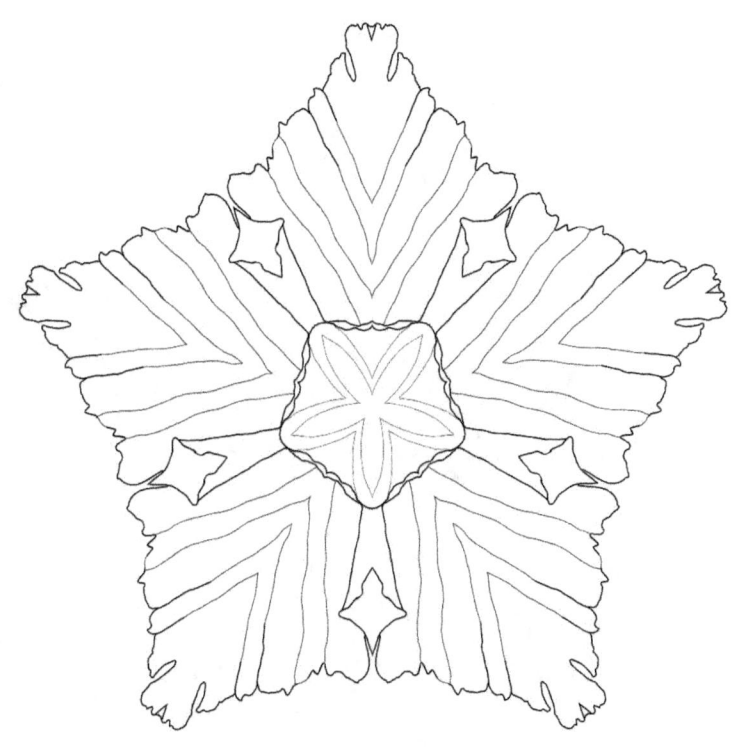

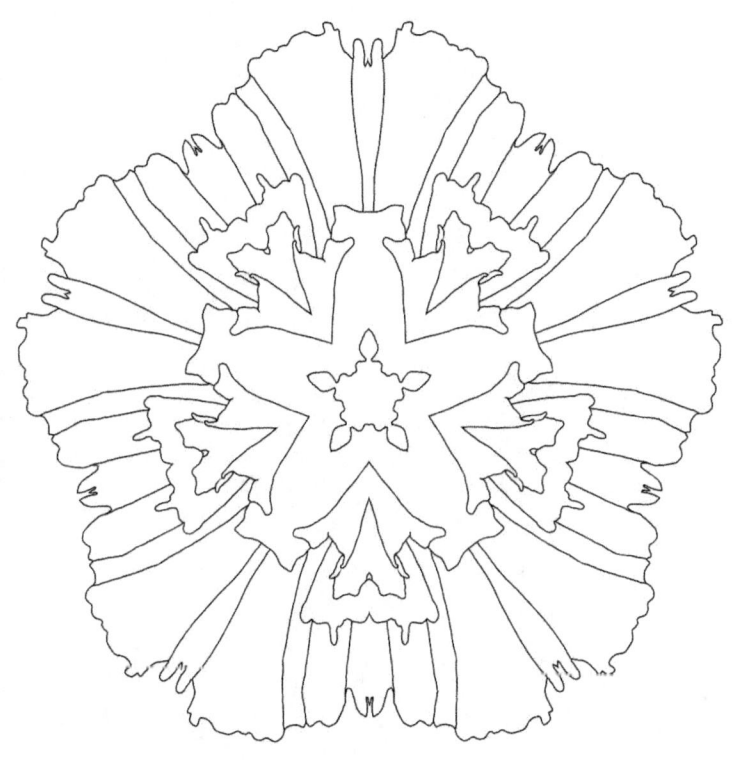

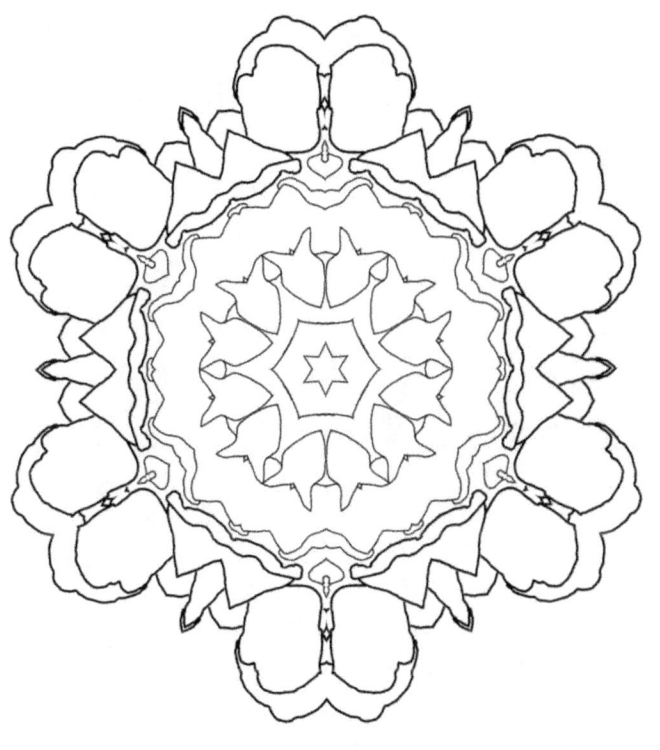

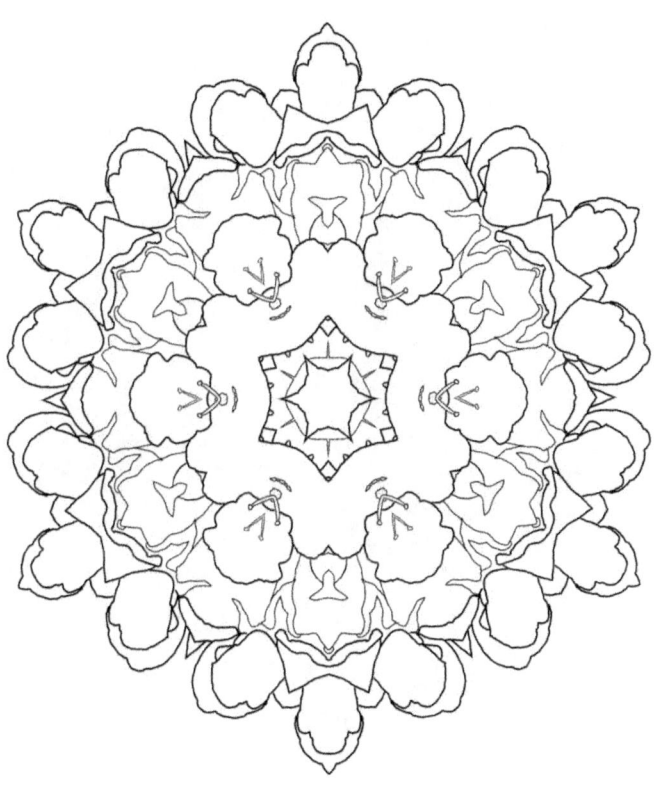

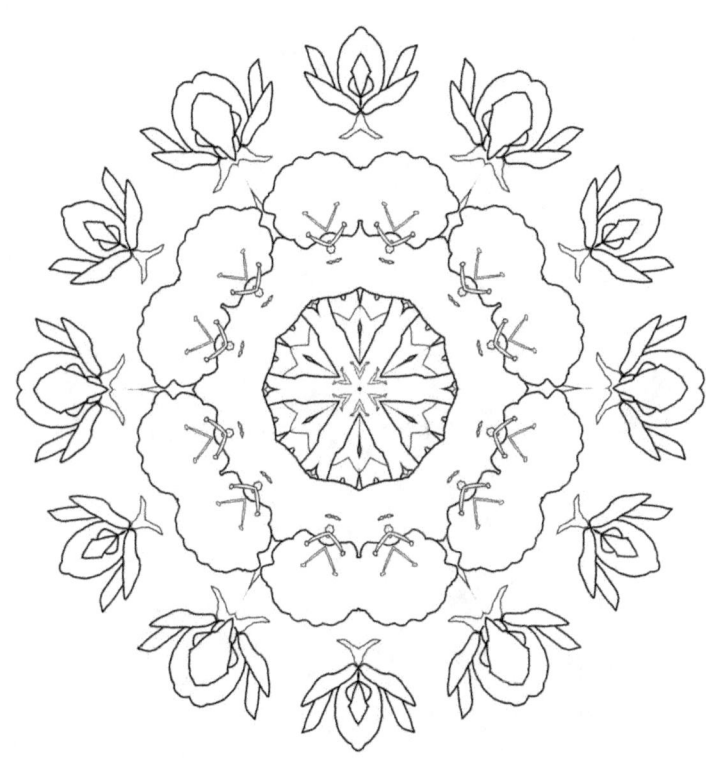

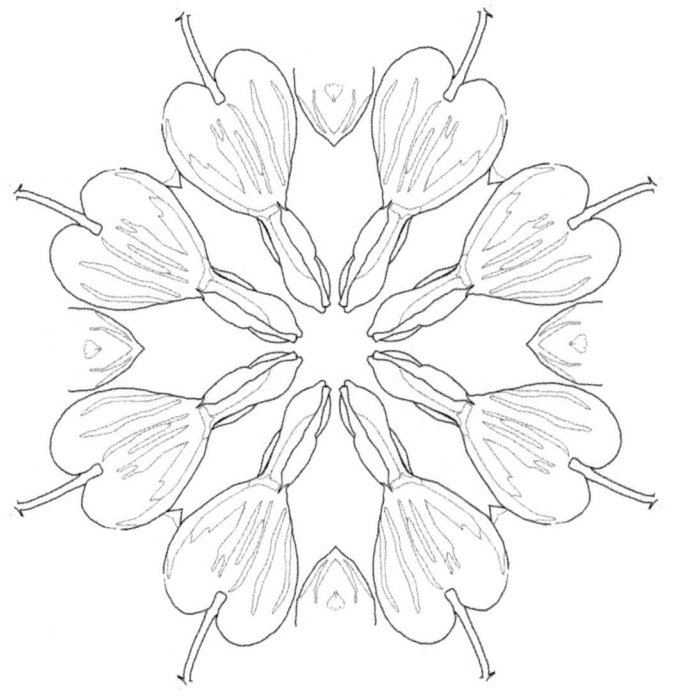

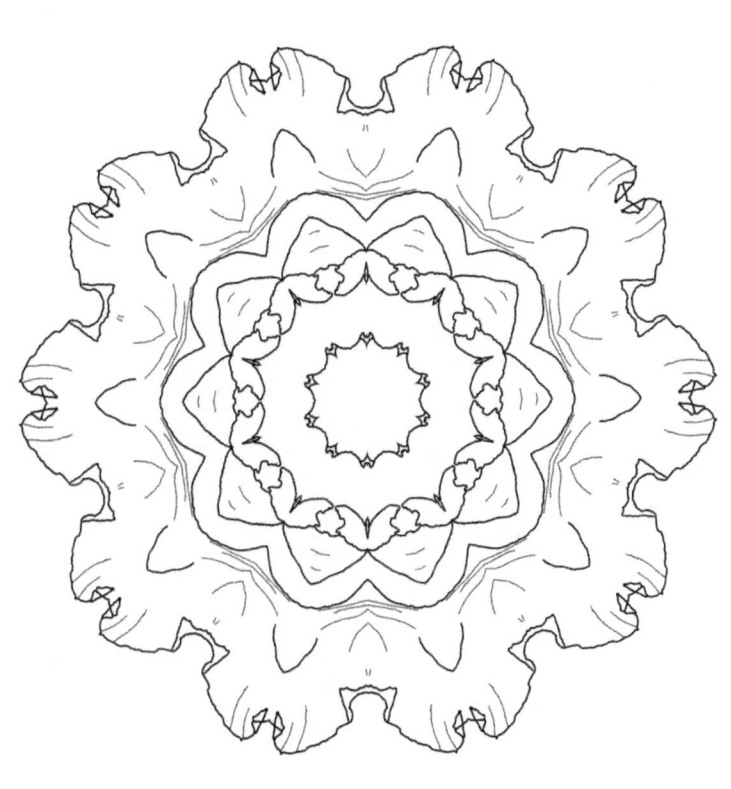

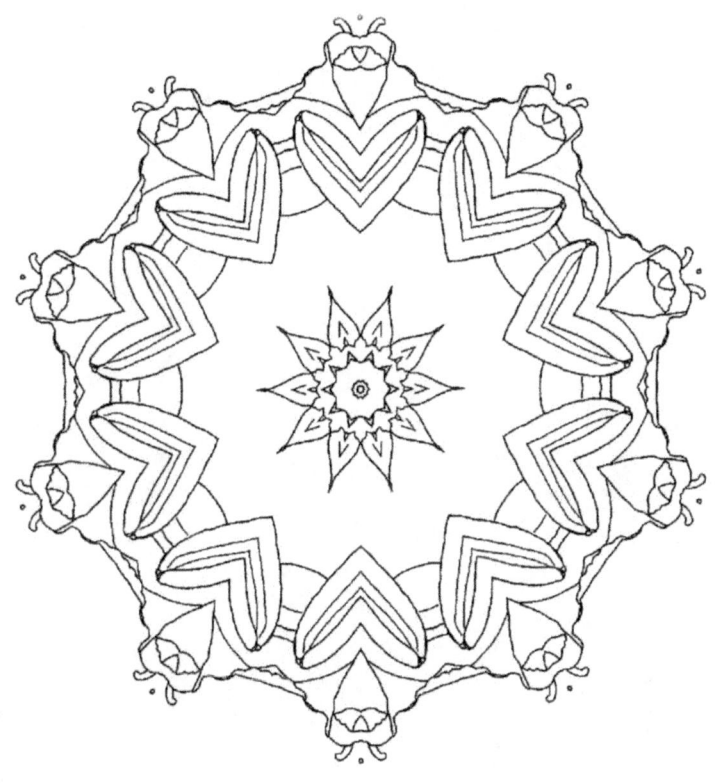

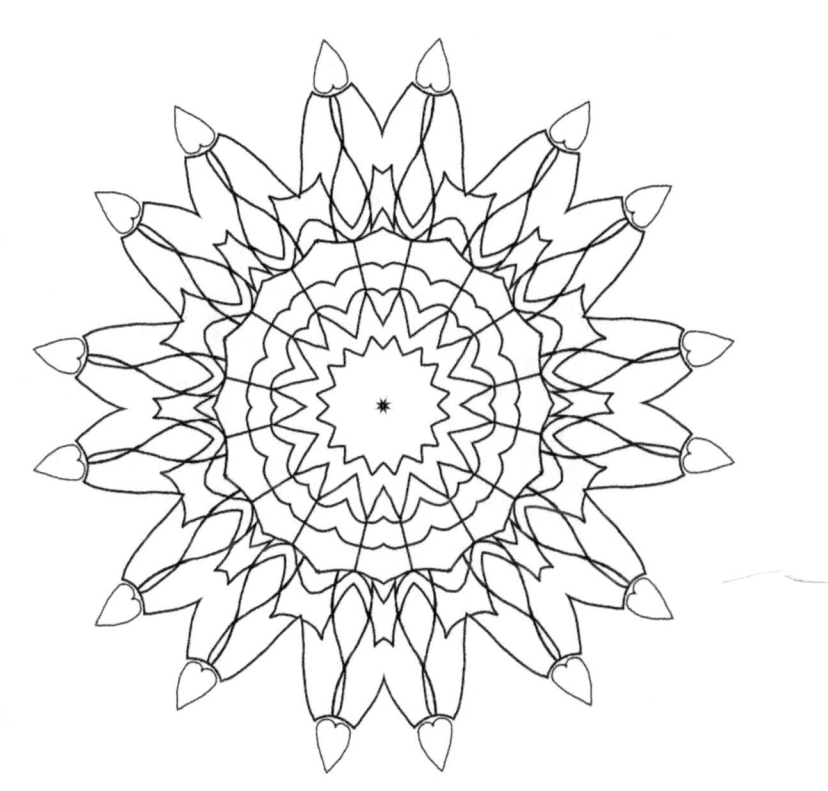

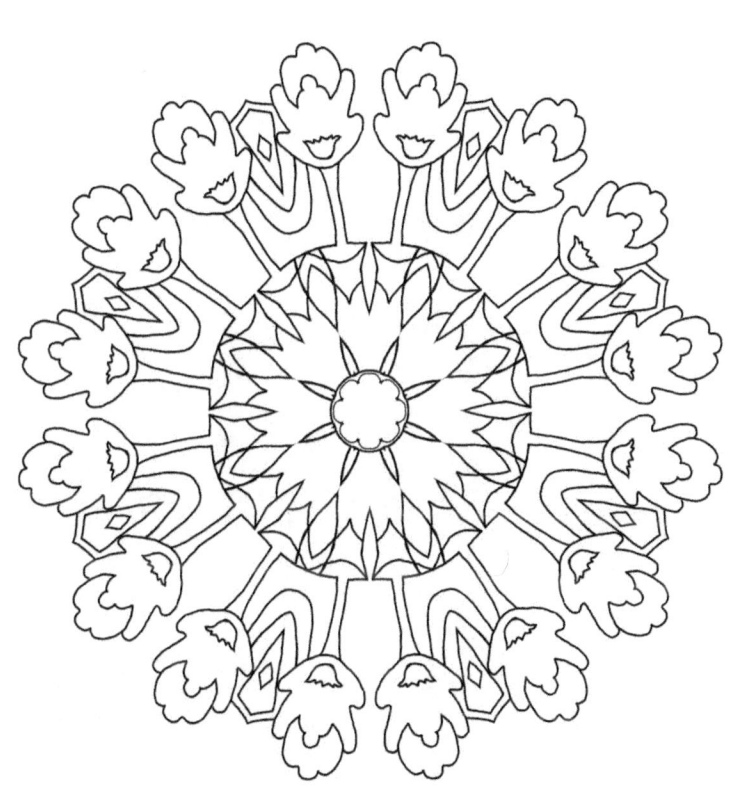

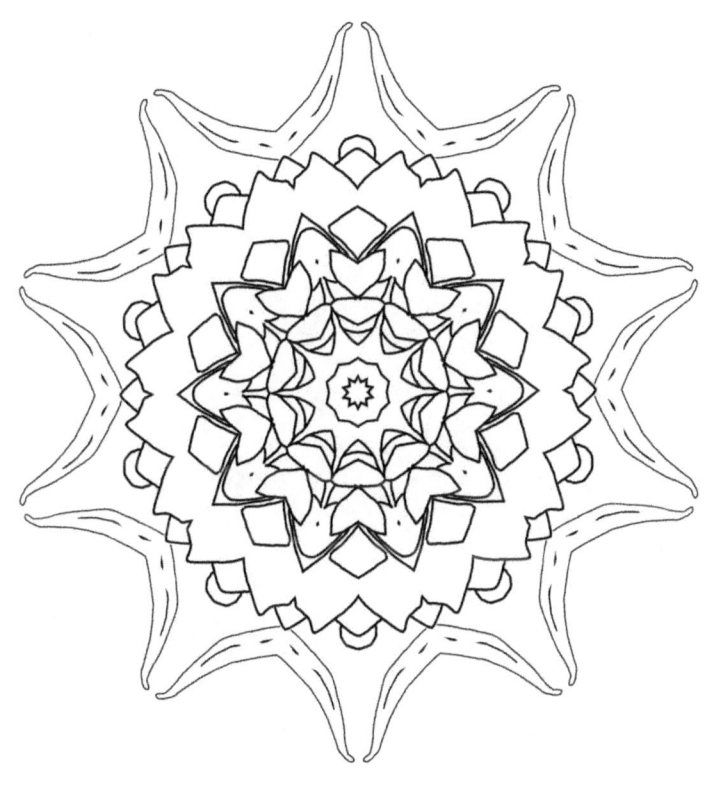

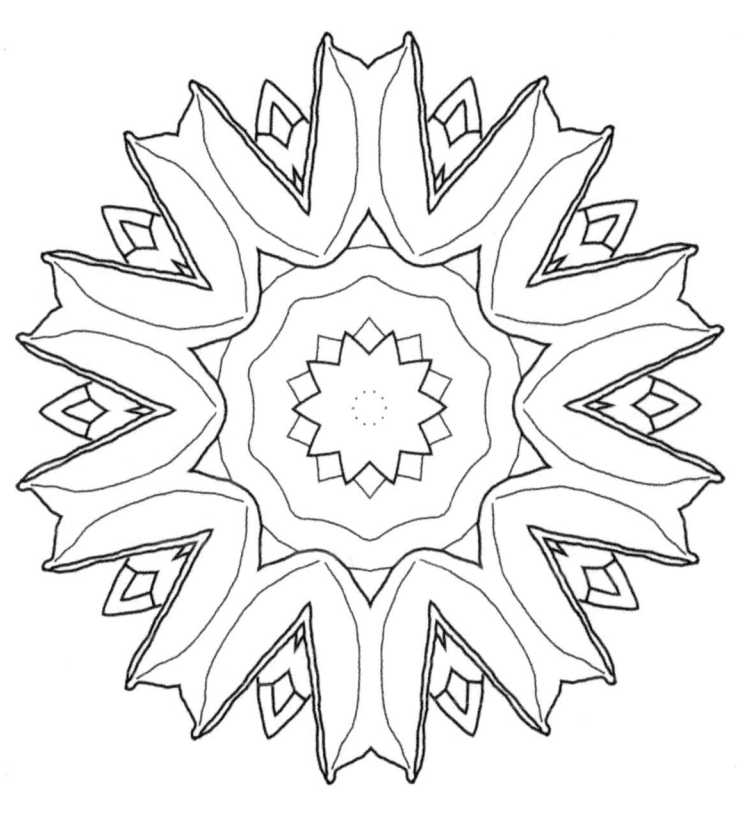

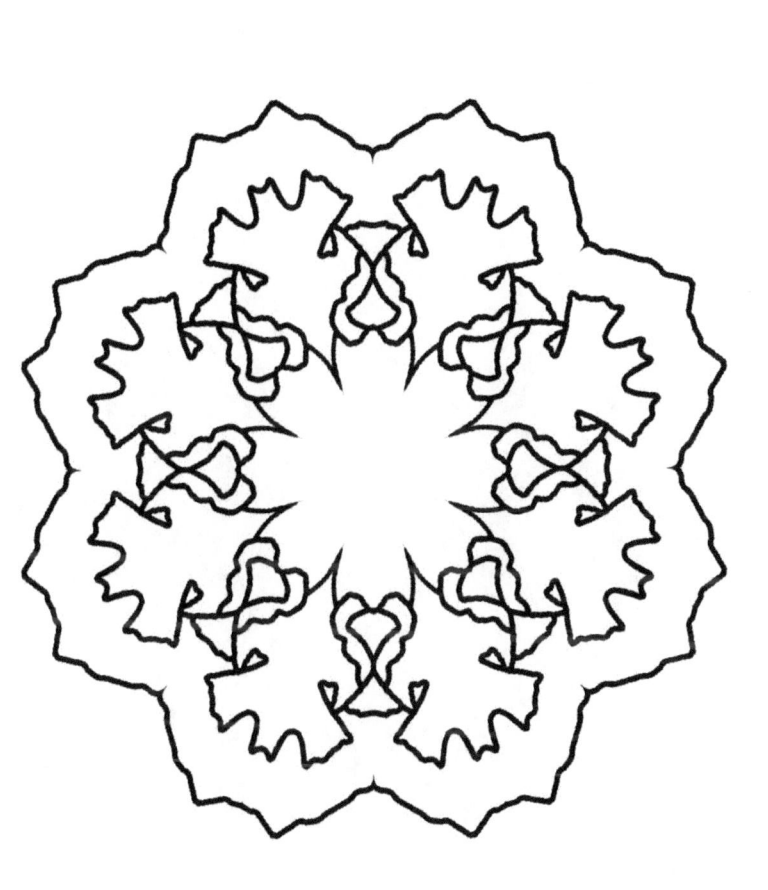

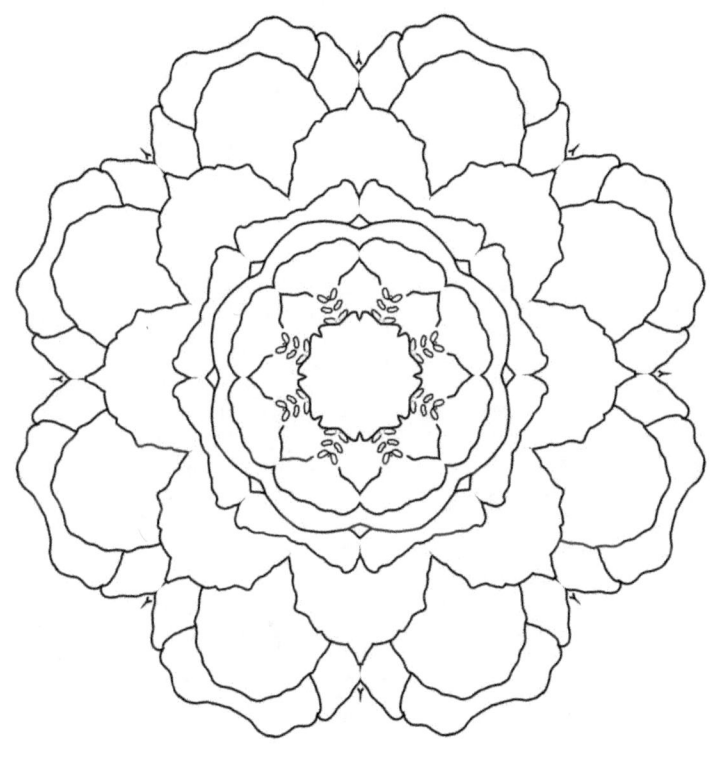

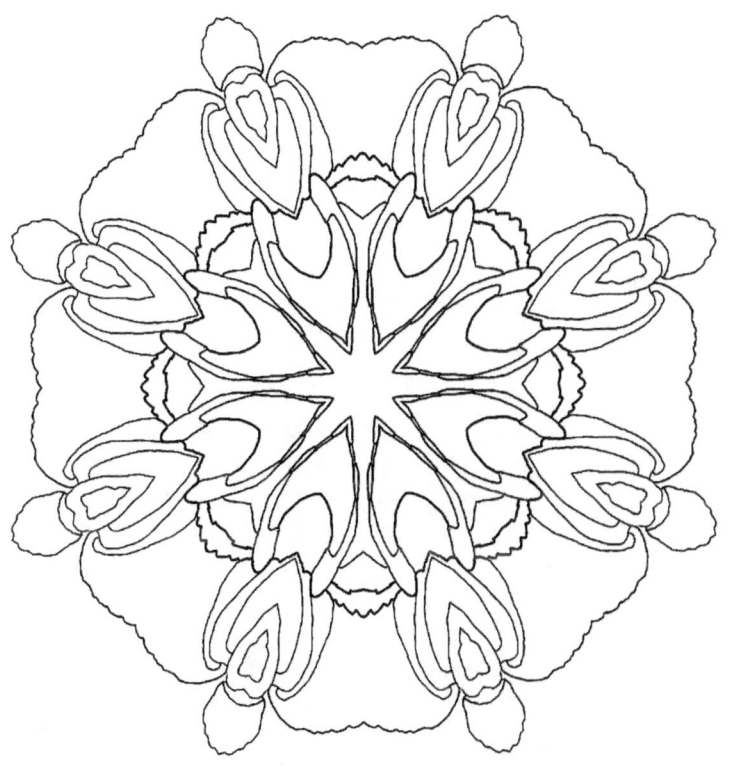

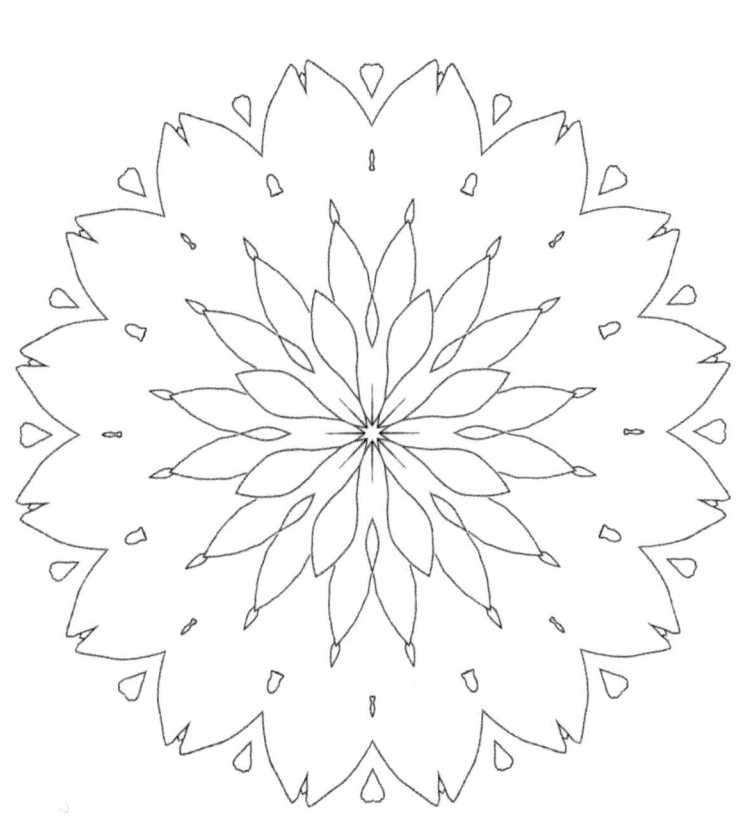

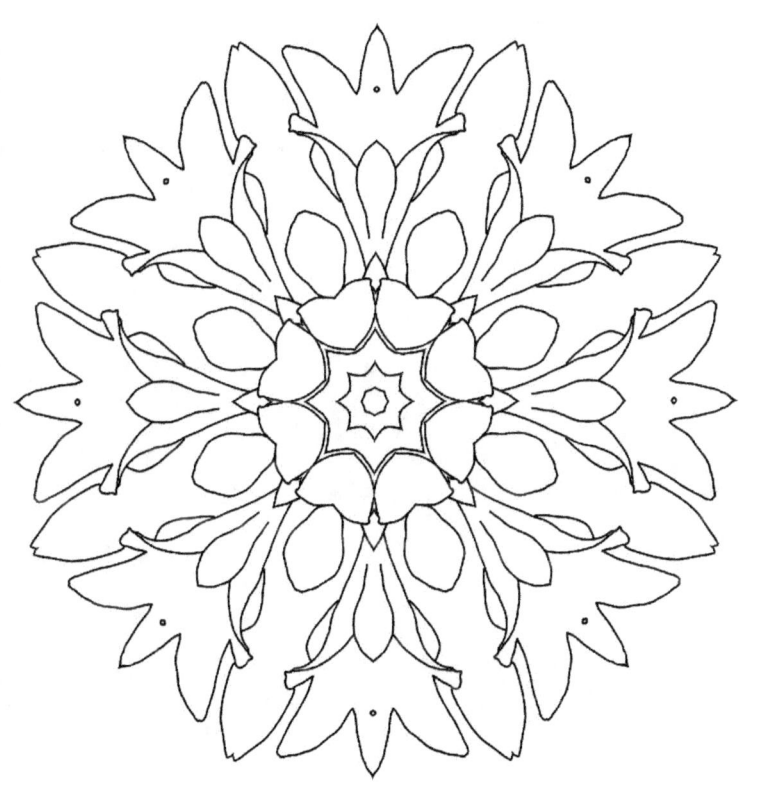

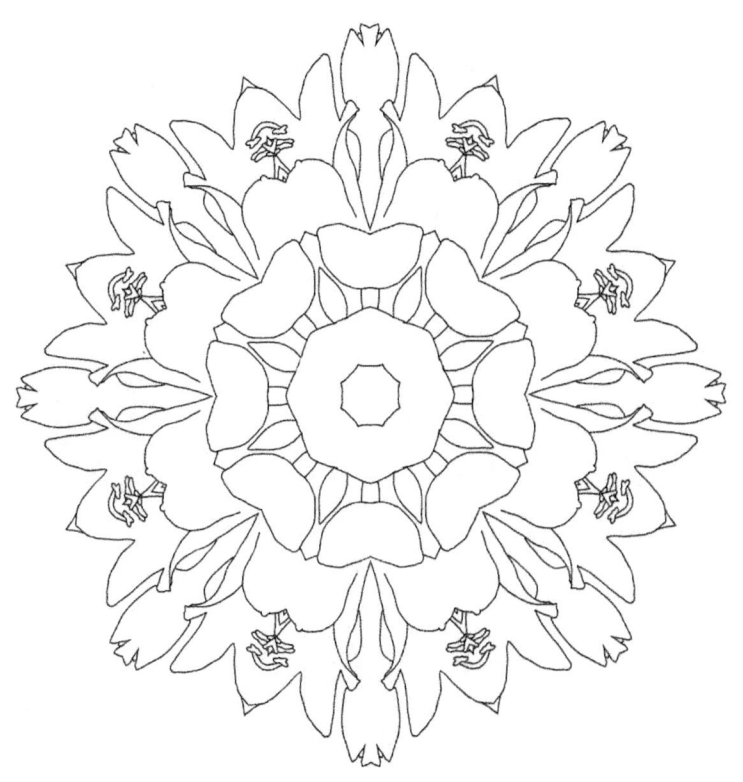

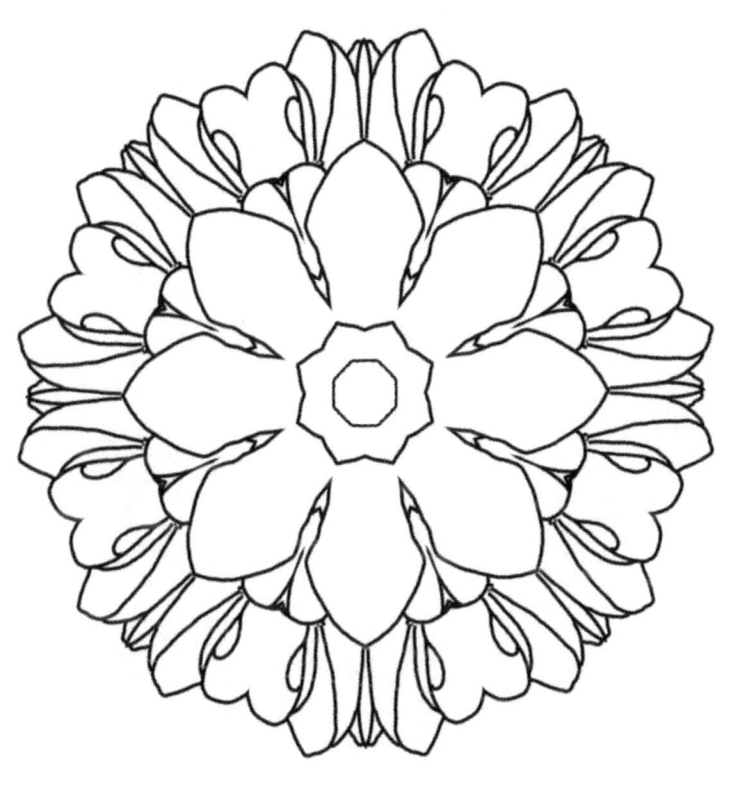

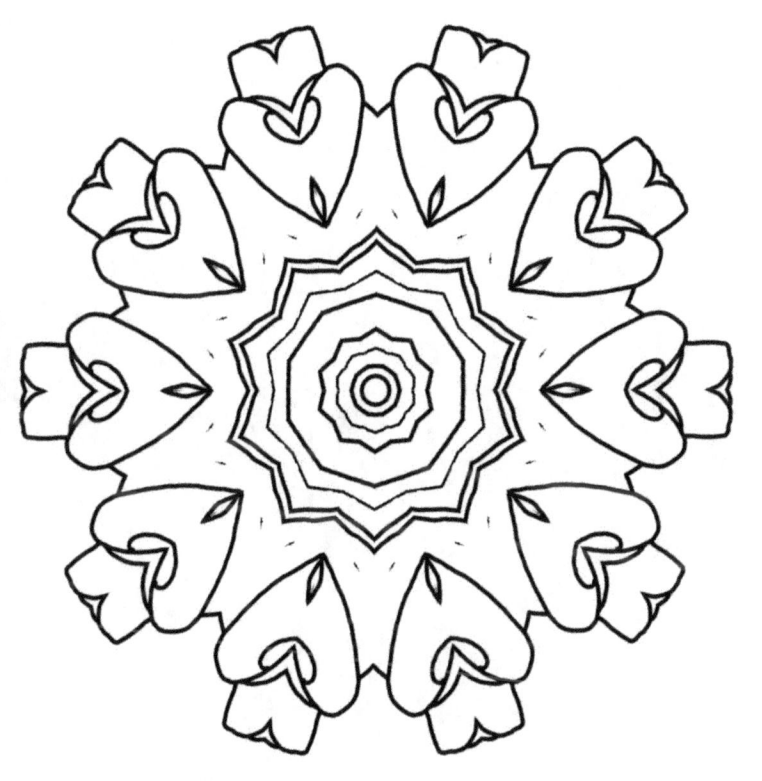

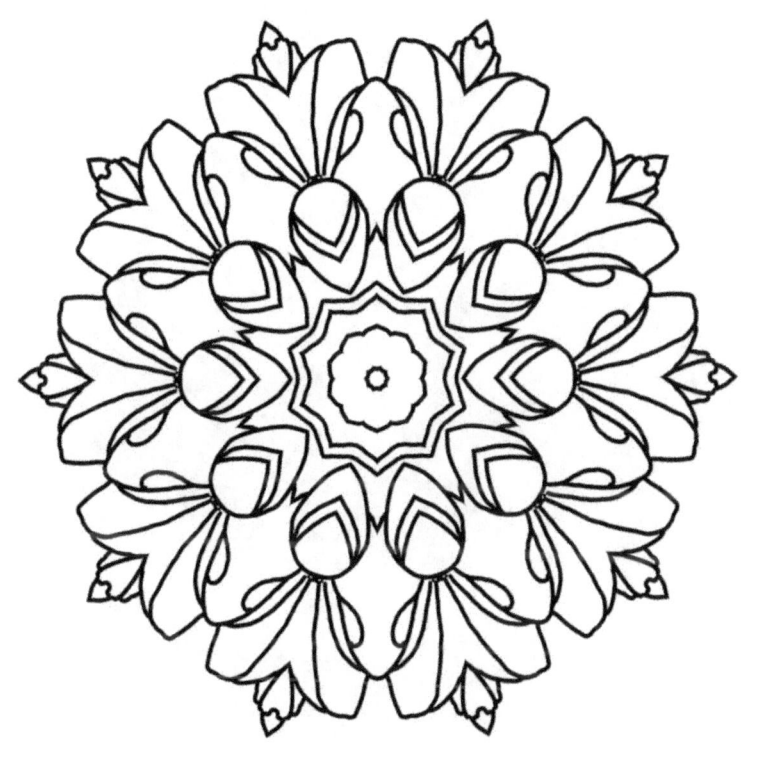

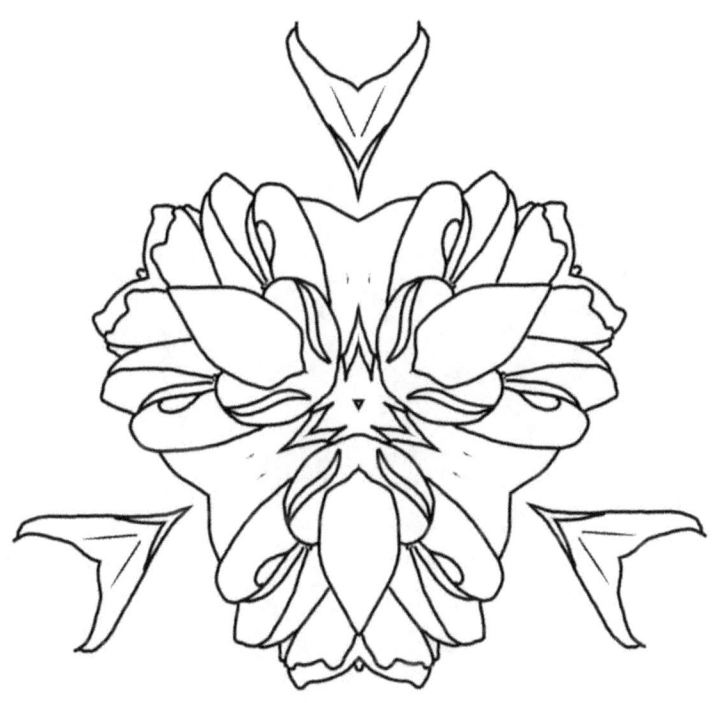

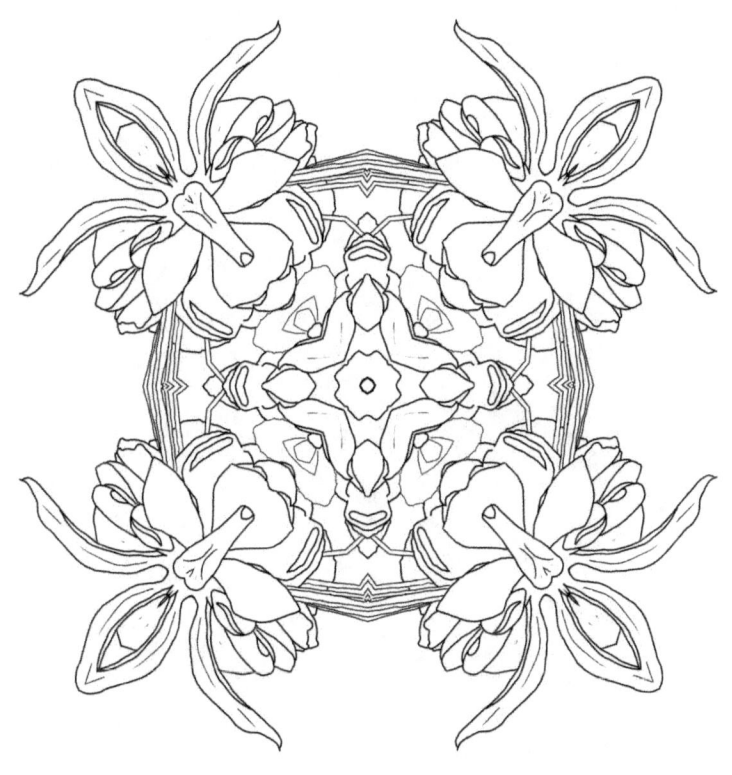

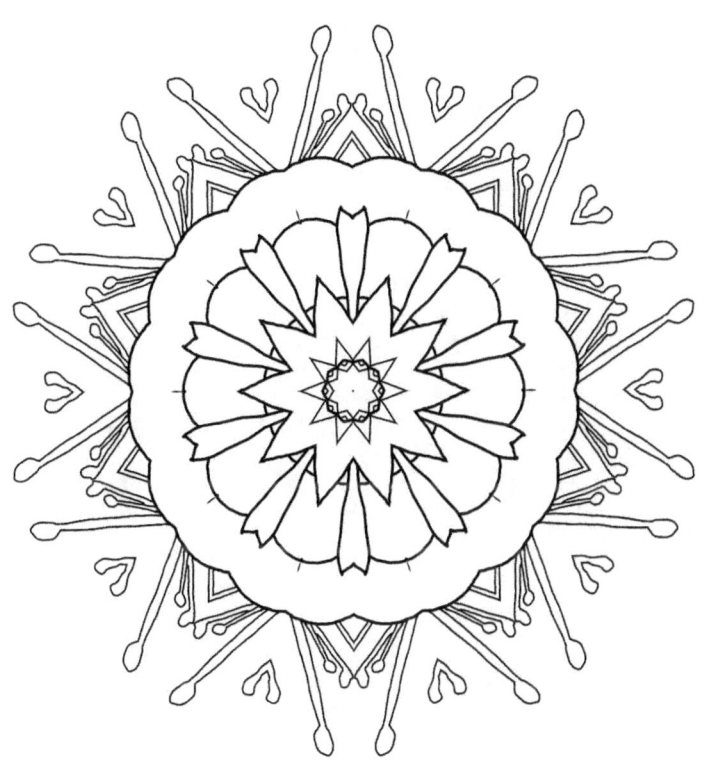

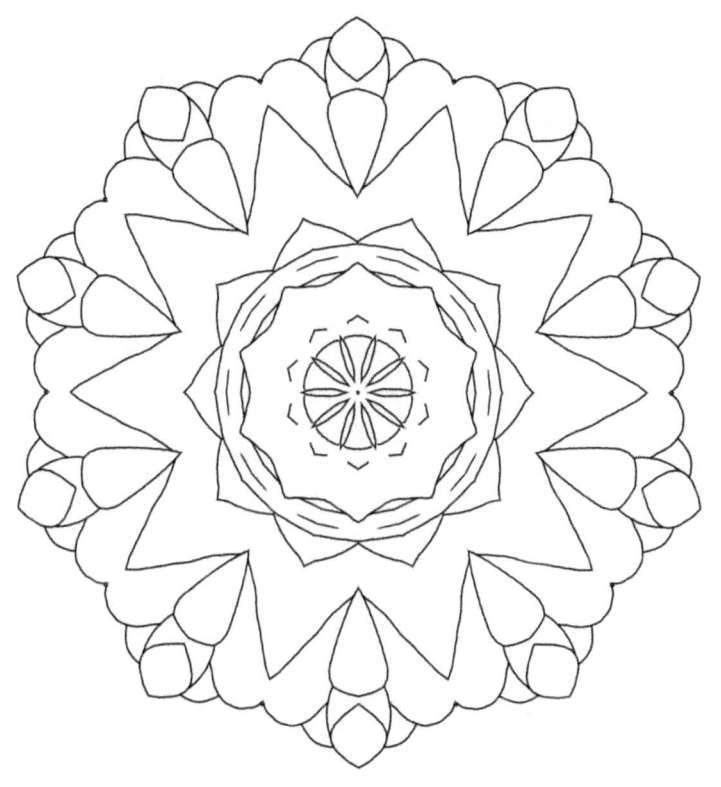

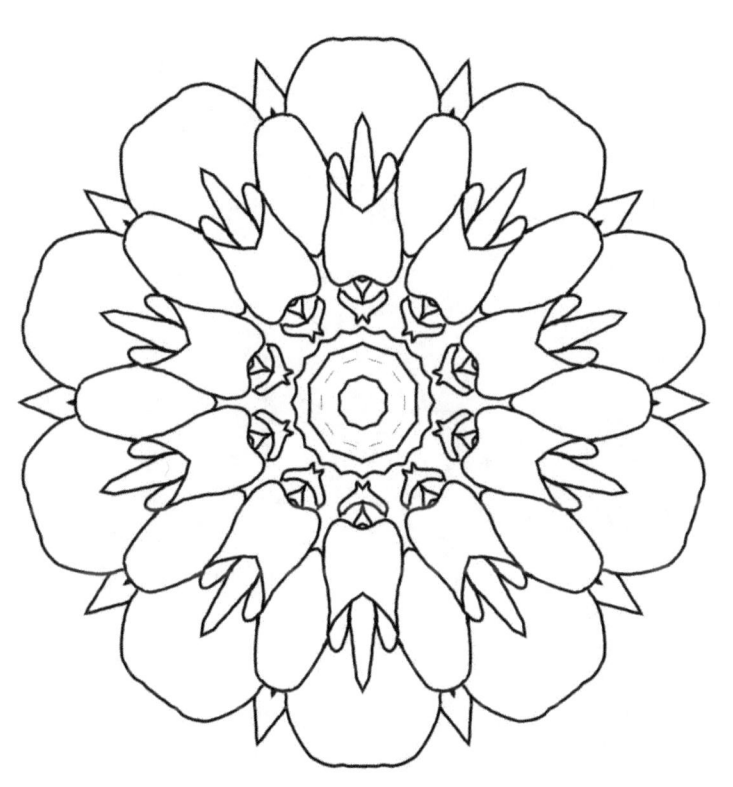

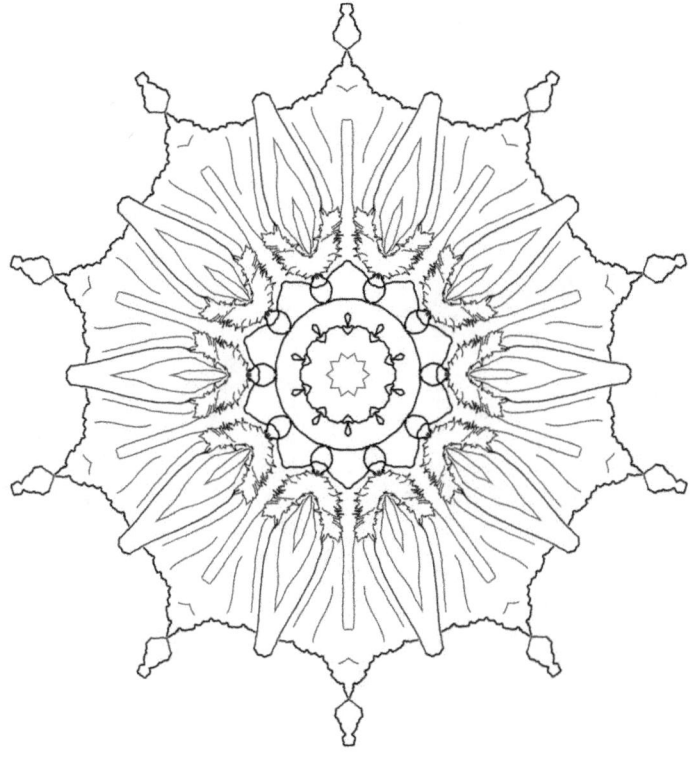

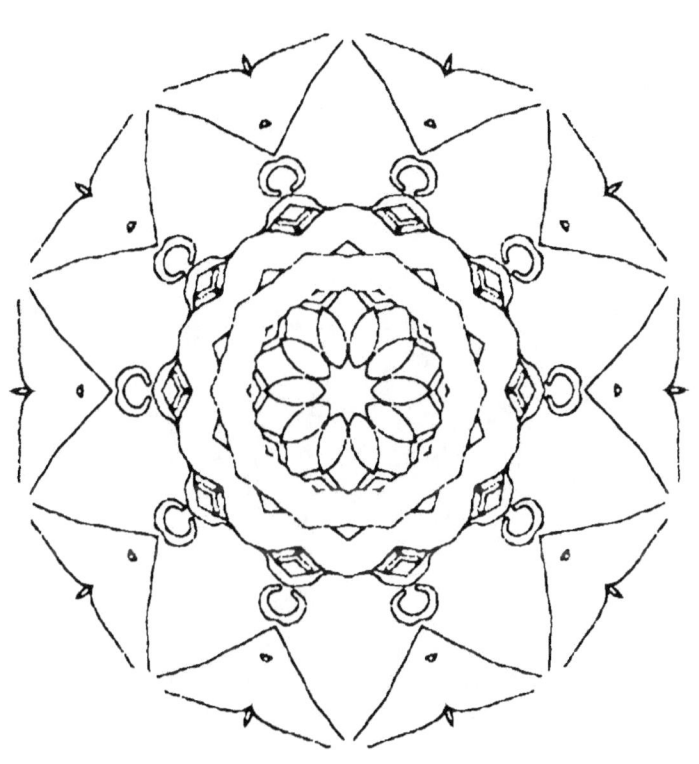

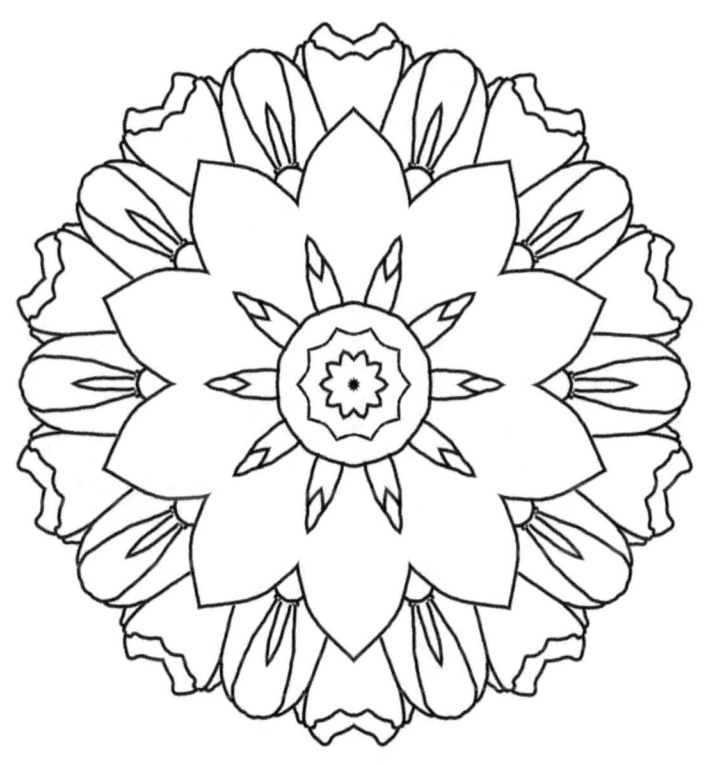

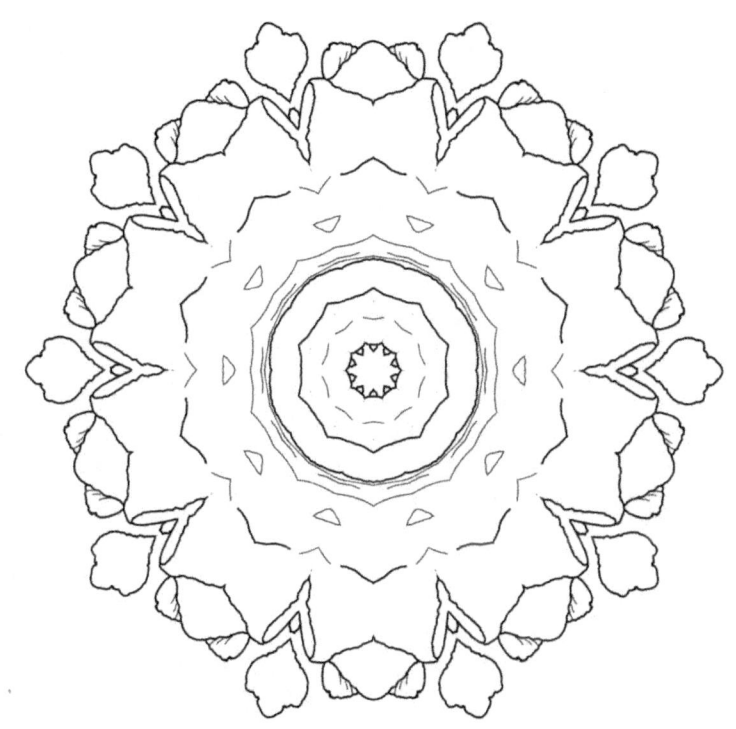

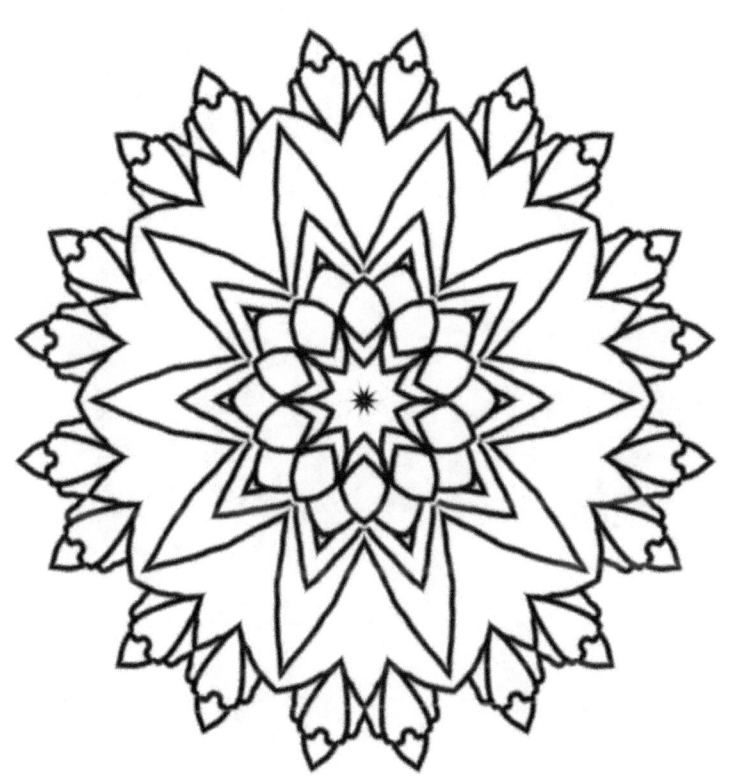

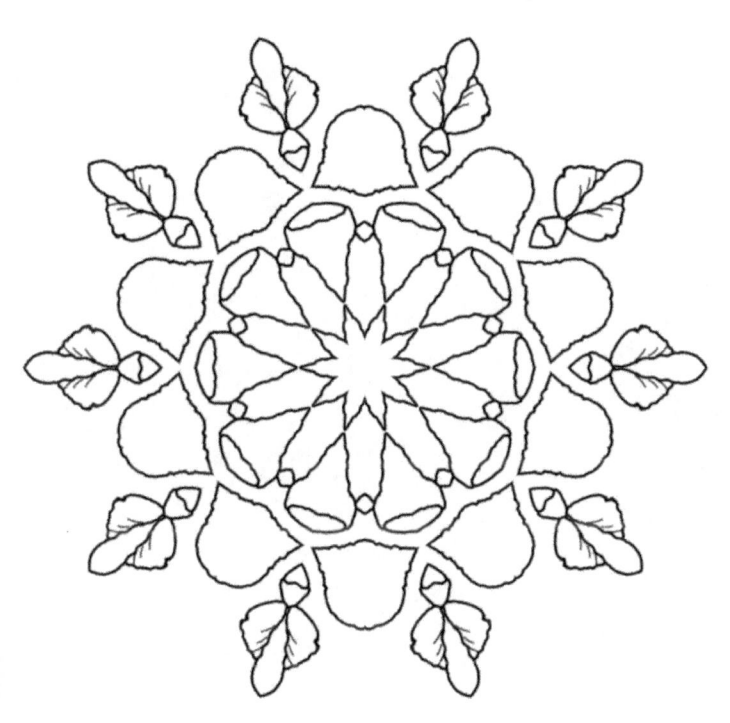